BRITAIN IN OLD  S

ALTRINCHAM

JOHN HUDSON

The History Press

First published in 1995
This edition first published in 2009

The History Press
The Mill, Brimscombe Port
Stroud, Gloucestershire, GL5 2QG
www.thehistorypress.co.uk

British Library Cataloguing in Publication Data.
A catalogue record for this book is available from the British Library.

ISBN 978 0 7524 5117 6

Typesetting and origination by The History Press
Printed in Great Britain

CONTENTS

INTRODUCTION

Though taking sidelong glances at Timperley, Hale and, in particular, Bowdon, this book strives to reflect chiefly on the past life of Altrincham, the ancient town that in 1990 celebrated the 700th anniversary of the granting of its charter. Those seven centuries have brought change far and above what might be regarded as natural progression. Most notably, the coming of the railway in 1849 saw the whole focus of the town centre switch away from the Market Place on the tops down to George Street, and later Stamford New Road. And from 1884, the name Broadheath came to signify less and less a drowsy hamlet on the way to Manchester, on the other side of the Duke of Bridgewater's canal, and increasingly an industrial estate which, by the inter-war years, was acclaimed as one of the great engineering workshops of northern England.

There had been industry in Altrincham before this, of course. A town could not live in the shadow of Manchester two hundred years ago without trying its hand at making cotton yarn and the machinery that kept the mills humming. The textile trade of Manchester was a world-renowned phenomenon, and a money-spinner on which none of its neighbouring communities could lightly turn their backs. Equally, a market town serving one of the most green and fruitful tracts of a green and fruitful county knew all about tinkering together ploughs and harrows and wagons, and rural industries were very much a part of the local equation by the time the railways came along.

Fortunately for those who know and love Altrincham as it is today, none of these pre-Broadheath industries impinged greatly on the area's leafy charms. By early in the nineteenth century it became clear that the communities north and south-east of Manchester would take the lion's share of the cotton trade, for better or worse; and as for the rural industries, all the major market towns in the country turned their hands to those, and they were scarcely the less appealing for it.

It meant that come the rail revolution in 1849, wealthy city merchants with an eye for the country life could choose with confidence to build a home in Altrincham. There was even hope of scaling the social ladder, with the lords of Dunham Park on the doorstep, and spreading out from them, the lesser and more accessible farmers and landowners who might give a personable and wealthy new neighbour an entrée into that elusive 'Cheshire set'. By the time the American engineer George Richards was blazing the trail at Broadheath little more than a hundred years ago, the social structure was set so apparently eternally in stone that the town could absorb the burgeoning industrial estate on its fringes without fearing for the future of its green

It meant that come the rail revolution in 1849, wealthy city merchants with an eye for the country life could choose with confidence to build a home in Altrincham. There was even hope of scaling the social ladder, with the lords of Dunham Park on the doorstep, and spreading out from them, the lesser and more accessible farmers and landowners who might give a personable and wealthy new neighbour an entrée into that elusive 'Cheshire set'. By the time the American engineer George Richards was blazing the trail at Broadheath little more than a hundred years ago, the social structure was set so apparently eternally in stone that the town could absorb the burgeoning industrial estate on its fringes without fearing for the future of its green spaces and leafy avenues.

With the merchants came the service industries to cater for them – the high-class grocers, the orchid growers, the carriage makers, the private schools whose influence on the town is still so apparent today. Walk through Altrincham at four o'clock on a schoolday afternoon and you will think half the world consists of teenage girls in blazers, micro-skirts, silk stockings and large clumpy boots, an intriguing mix of the masculine and feminine. Good for today's teachers for resisting the temptation to declare: 'No clumpy boots'. One recalls schoolmasters of a generation ago constantly conducting witch-hunts on passing fashions, usually a step behind the pace. 'No winkle-picker shoes', they would boom, when the most with-it kids in town had already graduated to chisel-toes.

In my choice of photographs I have tried hard to concentrate on human interest, and fear I might occasionally have offended would-be contributors in doing so. What I have tried to do is avoid good 1895 views of buildings that look like bad 1995 ones. Where possible, give me the carnival kings and queens, the Boys' Brigade campers playing up to the camera, the little boys running alongside the band. . . .

So do we regret the passing of the days relived with affection in these pages? I think that if we are honest with ourselves, we should not. What would the Edwardians have given for our warm homes, our shopping centres, our mobility? If we fail to capitalise on these advantages, even to begin to contemplate that society at that time was happier than it is today, then that is our fault, and not the result of the way the world has turned out.

Such thoughts should not lessen our enjoyment of looking back and wishing, in a vain and wistful way, that we could melt into the scenes that we recognise on these pages. Some, doubtless, would long to be in the crowd in Station Road for the coronation celebrations of 1911, or on the back row of the Regal on a warm summer's night. As I confess in the book, my wish would be simply to tramp the town centre of a century ago, living and breathing every sight and sound; it is little home-town streets like these, wherever we come from, that have helped to make us the way we are, and it is as well that we recognise this.

Because the images shown here are captured forever, fleeting moments held in time, it does not mean that the life they show was any more serene or predictable than ours. Seconds after the photographer had pressed the shutter the subjects of his picture were on their way – to miss their bus, stub their toe, burn the tea and do all the things that we do and wish we didn't. Perhaps they're all out there now, those forefathers of ours, looking down longing to sample our world of pizzas and Nintendos just as fervently as I would like to step into that picture of George Street and ask those three lads what on earth they are doing with that rocking chair.

John Hudson

SECTION ONE

HIGH DAYS AND HOLIDAYS

It is the summer of 1906, and large crowds throng the railway station approach to cheer the Earl of Stamford and his family on their return from the Midlands to live at Dunham Park. Advertising hoardings highlight some familiar names – the grocers Burston and Nixson, with branches at either end of Ashley Road in Altrincham and Sale, Kenna Smith's pianos, John Holt's builder's yard in Manor Road and Jewsbury and Brown, the big Manchester mineral water makers based on Ardwick Green. The policeman's helmet in the right foreground is interesting; not all forces favoured this angular style in Edwardian times, but a hat of a similar kind was worn nationally by the postmen of the day.

A detail of the picture opposite, showing off the summer fashions and capturing the straining anticipation of the spectators as the carriages approach. The Great Central Railway poster advertises excursions to Cleethorpes, via Sheffield, on several Sundays in July and August 1906, while trips to Llandudno and Birkenhead are publicised on the left. There are also advertisements for the Earl of Ellesmere's Collieries – and much more universally familiar, the dyers Pullars of Perth.

Altrincham Carnival's king and queen travel in style at the head of the procession in the
1920s, entering Railway Street from Stamford New Road, with Regent Road on the left.
The pub on this side of Regent Road is Tom Birtles' Woolpack Hotel, now no more; even
less in evidence today is the Stamford Hotel on the opposite corner, on a site now swamped
by a small part of the Graftons office and shops complex. The carnival raised money for the
General Hospital, and Ted Fleming and Freddie Fox are the best remembered king and queen,
but even enthusiasm evident in crowds of the size seen here could not save it from extinction.
Happily, since 1978, something of the spirit of the carnival has returned with the festival and
its big parade.

The carnival passing the other way down Railway Street in the 1920s. Behind the Wright's cotton textiles float is the Manchester and County Bank, now occupied by an art shop and office chambers that still bear the County name. Otherwise, the parade of shops includes a little café and a haberdashery, and such businesses as Malley and Adamson's and Hallett's.

Majorettes in the same carnival procession as on the previous page – or rather majorettes and
majors, for the dashing figures on the near side of the road are young men, niftily attired in
knee breeches and turbans. What a brave breed of youths Altrincham could boast in those
days, young men happy to endure the hoots of mirth of their pals and workmates for the sake
of communal dancing. It could be that they are fighting off the cold, here, too, for though the
sun is shining, most people in the crowd are well wrapped up.

Council chairman Councillor H. Smallwood plants a tree to mark the coronation of King George V and Queen Mary, 22 June 1911.

Market Street, and part of the morning procession to St George's Church to celebrate the 1911 coronation.

A dull day, but one fine enough for the king to be honoured with dignity: another view of the church parade in Market Street on coronation morning.

'Britannia' is the focal point in the more informal coronation afternoon procession, seen here in Railway Street.

Another view of the 1911 coronation afternoon procession.

Children from St George's Jubilee Schools dance round the maypole for the king, coronation afternoon, 1911.

In July 1946 King George VI and Queen Elizabeth visited the Churchill Machine Tool Company in Broadheath to honour its war effort, and the company's chairman and managing director, G.S. Maginness, is seen greeting them here. At one time some 1,500 people worked for the company at Broadheath, but takeovers by BSA in 1961 and Alfred Herberts in 1967 dealt severe blows to the Altrincham base. The Broadheath works finally closed in 1976, and by 1987 Churchill Machine Tools was no more.

VE-Day celebrations, Clifford Avenue, Timperley, May 1945. Lilian Williams, now Nash, of Derby Street, Altrincham, recalls tramping miles with a friend to collect the donkey from Warburton's on Moss Lane, only to return to be told off by her mother for being away for so long. In spite of food shortages, the donkey was brought in to be ridden by the little ones, rather than barbecued.

VE-Day, Clifford Avenue, Timperley, May 1945. The picture is familiar – women, children, and only old or very young men.

My fair ladies: Margaret Norris and Pamela Knox on the Garrick Theatre's Costumes Through the Ages float in Altrincham Festival's procession, 1982.

Section Two

Around the Town

Stamford New Road in Edwardian times.

Contrasting businesses in Stamford New Road at the time the picture opposite was taken.

23

Stamford New Road in about 1960, with the familiar no. 48 bus heading into town.

Above: Stylish headgear from Louie's, 1929. The 'backward glance' line does not seem very politically correct today.

Right: Skipper's cake shop at Orford House, Stamford Road, 1897. Apart from their rich and fruity cakes, they prided themselves on their pigeon pies.

Stamford New Road, late 1920s, with the sun blinds of the Co-op – or more precisely, the central Altrincham branch of the Manchester and Salford Equitable Co-operative Society Limited – prominent on the right. On this side of it are the swimming baths, opened in 1901 to mark Victoria's diamond jubilee, though the event coincided rather more closely with her death.

Altrincham . .
Electric Supply Limited,

ARE now, in their fifth year, supplying Current through a system of over 25 miles in length to something like 450 Consumers.

The Supply of Current is continuous day and night, and it may be used for Lighting, Heating, Motor Driving, &c., &c.

The Company undertake all **Installation Work,** as also Contracts for **Electric Bell Installations, Private Telephones, Cell Charging,** &c.

A large stock, representative of all the highest class of **Fittings, Electroliers, Bronzes** and **Fancy Glass Ware,** is available for inspection at our Showrooms, STAMFORD NEW ROAD. Telephone No. 52.

Estimates and all information as to the supply of Current may be had free on application there.

The Company further exchange, free of charge, all Lamps which may be burnt out or worn out in Installations which they have fitted.

Address all Enquiries to . .

Altrincham Electric Supply Limited,

A. FAIRLEY, Secretary,

Telephone No. 52. **STAMFORD NEW ROAD, ALTRINCHAM.**

The year is 1900, and 450 consumers are signed up with Altrincham Electric Supply Ltd in the company's fifth year of business.

Frederick Johnson's jeweller's shop in Railway Street, 1897. How he came to count the future Queen Alexandra among his customers is lost in history.

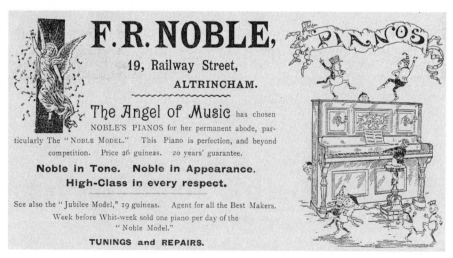

Noble in tone, high class in every respect – yet Noble's of Railway Street were still happy to have silly little dancing elves advertising their 26-guinea pianos in 1897. Since you could employ a live-in servant for rather less than 26 guineas a year a hundred years ago, the instruments were not cheap.

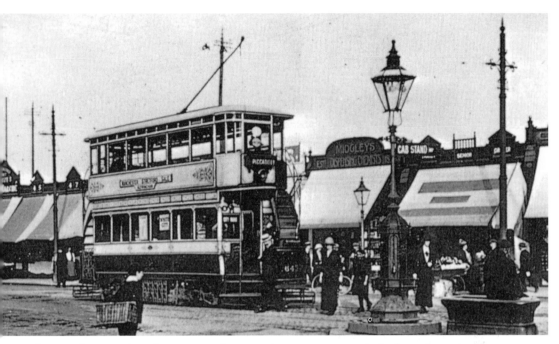

This is a famous Altrincham postcard image, the tram terminus in Railway Street in about 1909, with one of the new closed trams at the end of the line. On the left is the Bon Marché, dominating a parade of shops that to this day seems fragile and exotic for an inland town in the North of England, and must surely have appeared at least equally so then.

A drawing of the Bon Marché about a dozen years before the scene on the previous page. The owners had another draper's shop, simply trading as Wilson's, in the Jubilee Buildings on Stamford New Road.

The Market Place in 1858, when the top end was still the heart of the town.

The Old Market Place, *c*. 1960. This was traditionally a focal point for wayside inns – the Red Lion and Horse and Jockey, now gone, the Orange Tree, still with us and larger than formerly, and the imposing Unicorn, trading these days as the Hogshead.

The splendid mock-Tudor Lloyds Bank in the Old Market Place in about 1910, with the Red Lion on the right. The latter building is now occupied by the Shere Khan Indian Restaurant.

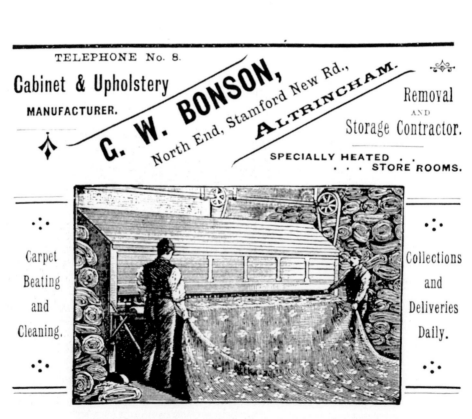

TELEPHONE No. 8.

Cabinet & Upholstery

MANUFACTURER.

G. W. BONSON,

North End, Stamford New Rd.,

ALTRINCHAM.

Removal

AND

Storage Contractor.

SPECIALLY HEATED . .

. . . STORE ROOMS.

Carpet Beating and Cleaning.

Collections and Deliveries Daily.

It looks as if Bonson's were kept busy beating and cleaning carpets – look at the piles of them on either side of that fearsome-looking machine.

GEORGE THORNELY,
SADDLE AND HARNESS MAKER,
20, MARKET PLACE, ALTRINCHAM.

In returning thanks to the Public in general for the very liberal support he has received in the above Business, begs to inform them that he has always a large Assortment of Saddles, Harness, Horse Clothing, Brushes, &c., in Stock. Every description of Repairs executed with good Workmanship and despatch.

G. T's. Saddlery business being the Oldest established in Town, begs for an inspection of his STOCK.

Gentlemen's Saddles, Harness &c. bought or taken in Exchange.

EVERY DESCRIPTION OF
New and Second-hand Harness, always in Stock.

Trading from different addresses in the Market Place, George Thornely had fingers in two plump pies in the 1850s.

G. THORNELY,
CLOCK & WATCHMAKER,
JEWELLER, &c.,
No. 12, MARKET PLACE, ALTRINCHAM.

In returning thanks to the Gentry and Public, for the very liberal support he has received since commencing the above Business, begs to remind them that he is the only Practical Clock Maker and Repairer in the neighbourhood; Clocks and Watches Cleaned and Repaired on his own Premises, by Experienced Workmen.

CLOCKS, WATCHES, JEWELLERY &C.
Always in Stock in great variety.

Clocks Wound up, and Regulated by yearly contract.

A
Five=Guinea
Raincoat
for
69/6

Byroms are offering a small stock of Mandleberg's best quality Raincoats at 69/6 each, instead of the usual price of five guineas.

They are made from the same material that was used for the Scott Antarctic Expedition. The toughest, smartest, most rainproof fabric in the world.

Call in and see them in the New Tailoring Showroom at

BYROMS Men's Shop
8 & 10, KINGSWAY, ALTRINCHAM
THE LARGEST & OLDEST STORE IN THE DISTRICT

With men in mind, Byroms of Kingsway adopted the rugged approach in 1933. The selling line extolling the material used in Scott's Antarctic expedition might have been more effective had not the participants in that ill-fated venture perished of cold.

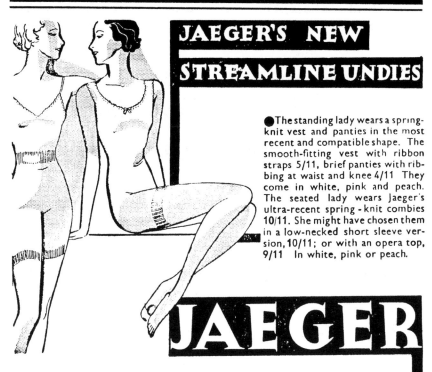

JAEGER'S NEW STREAMLINE UNDIES

●The standing lady wears a spring-knit vest and panties in the most recent and compatible shape. The smooth-fitting vest with ribbon straps 5/11, brief panties with ribbing at waist and knee 4/11 They come in white, pink and peach. The seated lady wears Jaeger's ultra-recent spring-knit combies 10/11. She might have chosen them in a low-necked short sleeve version, 10/11; or with an opera top, 9/11 In white, pink or peach.

JAEGER

SOLD BY:

BYROMS of KINGSWAY, ALTRINCHAM

The Oldest and Largest Store in the District

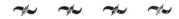

A TRANSFORMATION SCENE

Byroms have considerably extended their premises by making three new large showrooms of the old Garrick headquarters.

They are well worth a visit of inspection!

With women in mind, Byroms took the softly-softly approach in 1932, with much talk of streamlined 'panties' and 'combies' in white, pink or peach. It is interesting to note that the shop was able to expand as a result of the Garrick Theatre opening their new HQ on Barrington Road.

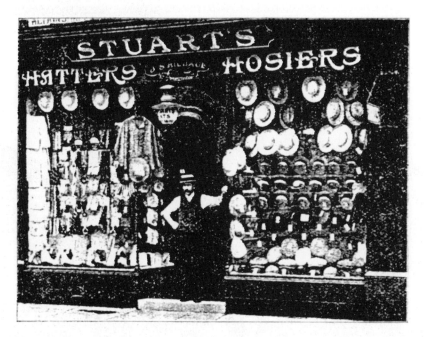

Everthing for Men's Wear.

—o—

Latest and Best Styles of Hats.

—o—

TRY OUR FAMOUS 3s. 11d. HATS.

✻✻✻✻✻✻✻✻✻✻✻✻✻✻✻✻✻

Stuarts,
115, George Street,
Altrincham.

PROPRIETOR:
J. S. HILDAGE.   'Phone 771 Alt.

A Stuart's advertisement from 1911, when a hat cost 3s 11d.

The classic view, George Street in the late 19th century, when it was the unrivalled commercial heart of the town. With the busy advertising hoardings on the left, it is the scene every present-day son and daughter of Altrincham would like to walk back into if they had a time machine – if only to ask the three boys under Scales' sign what they are doing with that rocking chair.

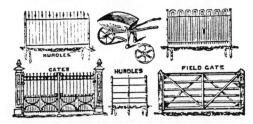
Ironmongers who could turn their hand to a little tinsmithing and cobbling-together in the days when gadgets were produced locally, rather than bought off-the-peg, were constantly in demand – and in 1900, Edwin Watson, with shops and workshops here and there, must have thought he had everything well in hand.

The technical school in George Street in 1904, pictured by the local photographer Thornton. The Tech was in the library building that was demolished in 1975, though the school had moved out decades before, in 1923, when it transferred to Navigation Road.

William Shuttleworth's was a popular George Street business in Victorian times, a baker's and grocer's that also dealt in wines and spirits. In the days when Altrincham Agricultural Show was widely regarded as the biggest and best one-day event of its kind, it was often Shuttleworth's that walked off with the butter prizes.

The library and technical school in George Street, 1911. The local board of health took over the venture in 1877, and enlarged it to include the Tech in 1892.

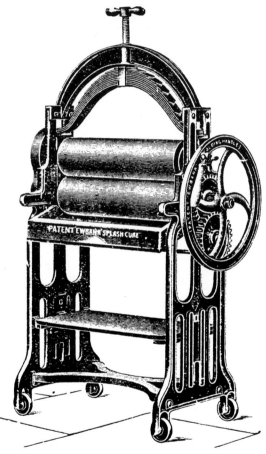
Filmer's, another big ironmonger's on George Street, 1911. The mangle illustrated is a Ewbank Patent Splash Cure.

LITHERLAND BROS.

COACH BUILDERS, &c.

Rubber Tyres a Speciality.

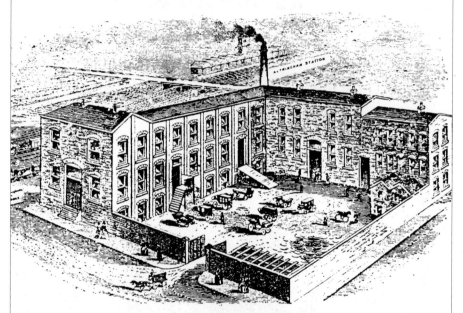

Litherland's Central Carriage Works, Altrincham.

Motor Cars Trimmed and Painted by Experienced Workmen ❧ ❧

CAPE HOODS, APRONS & DASHES FITTED

CENTRAL CARRIAGE WORKS,

Manor Road, Altrincham.

Litherland's Central Carriage Works in Manor Road in 1911, when the balance between horse-drawn and motorised transport was still fine. Litherland's very sensibly kept feet in both camps until it was clear that the horseless carriage was the transport of the future.

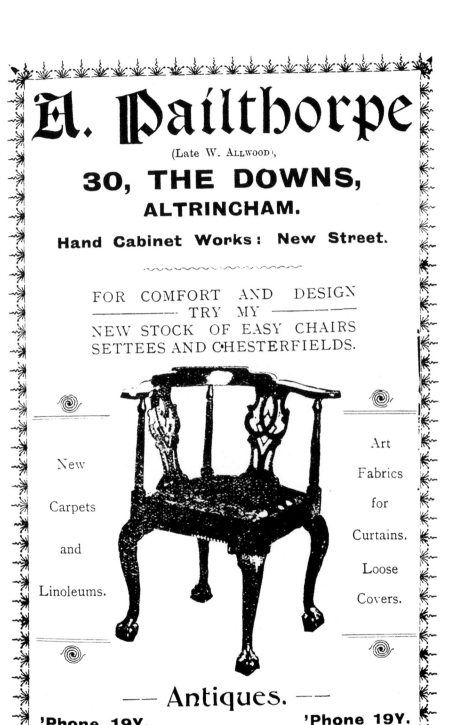

Cabinetmakers, like ironmongers, were thick on the ground, though few could quote a telephone number as catchy as Altrincham 19Y. What price some of Pailthorpe's antiques today?

The get-up looks smart enough, but we could live without the self-satisfied grin. Advertising from the days when God made them high or lowly, and ordered their estate.

SECTION THREE

IT'S GREAT TO BE YOUNG

Unidentified Altrincham girls with two nursemaids, photographed by the town's Duke Dawson studio in the 1920s.

Navigation Road children: above, boys with Union flags celebrating the first Armistice in November 1918, and below, a group of girls and their teachers some four years later.

Smart lads: Standard VII, St Vincent's School, October 1931.

Culcheth Hall School for girls in Ashley Road was started by the Lang family on 12 February 1891, and had the presence of mind to have the scene photographed when they welcomed their first 13 pupils. They must have felt especially grateful to Mr and Mrs Zimmerman, whose daughters Elsie, Florence, Nessie and May made up almost a third of their total roll.

Culcheth Hall School in the mid-1890s, considerably grown from the picture on the previous page. This photograph is from the time of the first principal, Miss Helen Lang, who stepped down in 1897.

Culcheth Hall's housewifery and science room in Edwardian times. The blackboard spells out the lesson for the day – grilling steak and chops and preparing chipped potatoes.

Ten o'clock on a sunny morning in Culcheth Hall's Upper III classroom at around the end of the First World War. You can almost smell the ink and polish, but colourful history and travel pictures brighten the wall, and there are flowers on the bookcase.

Junior pupils at Loreto Convent, June 1940. The school, now a major independent grammar school for girls, was founded in 1909 and has been at its now vastly expanded Dunham Road site since 1913.

Senior girls at Loreto Convent in the summer of 1940.

The 2nd Altrincham Boys' Brigade, attached to the Methodist Church, was founded in 1902 and is the oldest youth group in the town – pre-dating the Scouts, and boasting a record of continuous service that the disbanded and re-formed 1st Altrincham cannot match. This is the cookhouse squad at the brigade's camp at Rhyl in May 1928.

Playing up to the press photographer, Rhyl, 31 May 1928.

Ducking Arthur Garforth, Rhyl, 1928.

The 2nd Altrincham Boys' Brigade canteen's regular customers, Rhyl, May 1928.

High jinks, boxing gloves and a woman's dress at the 2nd Altrincham's camp at Skegness, 1925.

2nd Altrincham Boys' Brigade Founders' Day in 1947, processing to the chapel in Borough Road. It is a scene of post-war austerity, enlivened only by the knot of little boys running alongside the parade. There were once 16 Methodist societies in Altrincham, and Borough Road was at the forefront of moves to unite the surviving chapels some 30 years ago. It held its last service in August 1966, joining other congregations at Bank Street until the movement's splendid new church and meeting place was opened in Barrington Road two years later.

Youngsters from the 1st, 2nd and 7th Altrincham at the Boys' Brigade's joint section arts and crafts show in November 1978. From left to right are Stephen Cooper, Sandy Marshall, Sion Wynn, Ian Blackburn, Ian Miller, Christopher Greaves and Alan Richardson.

The 2nd Altrincham Boys' Brigade members who won the battalion drill competition at Carrington Lane Methodist Hall – none of them looking more pleased than their leader on the right, David Bowyer.

Marching youth groups in the Mayor's Parade, 1974.

Altrincham Festival marchers, July 1978.

2nd Altrincham Boys' Brigade members off to camp at Great Yarmouth, 1972. Smiling at the camera are Bernard Gibbon, Ken Bailey and Chris Burgess.

Section Four

Leafy and Suburban

Deer at Dunham Park some 60 years ago.

From the same period, the much loved Old Mill at Dunham Park.

A pretty view from Dunham Park showing the Green Walk.

Autumn peace at Dunham Park just before the First World War.

Mind the traffic: Dunham Hill in about 1910.

The bird sanctuary at Castle Mill in the 1920s, with its memorial to a member of the Coward family of Bowdon. Another member of the family, Thomas Alfred Coward, is remembered for his book *Picturesque Cheshire*, a phrase that certainly encapsulates the view seen here.

Altrincham and Bowdon's war memorial piled high with flowers on a late autumn afternoon in the 1920s, when the Remembrance Day service still stirred painful memories for thousands locally.

Sunshine, shadows and just a smattering of traffic: New Chester Road in the late 1950s.

A scene from suburban life: packing the car at Graysands Road, spring 1955.

JOHN ROBSON

NURSERYMAN, SEEDSMAN, AND

LANDSCAPE GARDENER,

Invites inspection of his stock of

ORCHIDS.

The Finest Collection in the trade in the neighbourhood
of Manchester.

Palms, Stove and Greenhouse Plants, Pot Roses, Shrubs, Fruit and Forest Trees, and Herbaceous Plants.

All kinds of Floral Decorations carried out.   *Estimates Free.*

Seed Warehouse : 27, The Downs, Altrincham.
Nurseries : Hale Road, Altrincham.
TELEPHONES: SHOP, 166; NURSERIES, 166a.

In 1911, orchids were a must in suburban drawing rooms. Mr Robson's use of the phrase 'landscape gardener' seems surprisingly modern.

Not too much stirring in Ashley Road on this sunny day in the 1920s.

Burston and Nixson's, who had shops at both the Altrincham and Hale ends of Ashley Road, prided themselves on the quality of all manner of 'provisions', but this advertisement from 1911 stresses the variety of their hams. If the drawing pictures an actual member of their staff, doubtless his friends teased him as being the biggest ham of all.

Four friends resting and taking a picnic after some rather well-dressed work in the garden, Groby Road, April 1948.

Above: Susan Fairley, aged four, revives seaside memories in her garden in Graysands Road, spring 1955.

Right: John David Fairley, aged six, brings a hint of the Old West to suburban Graysands Road in early 1955. A year later the little boys of Altrincham, and in truth most of the rest of the western world, had swapped their cowboy outfits for Davy Crockett hats.

Feeding the ducks in Stamford Park, September 1952. Municipal parks are not what they used to be but, against the odds, the descendants of these birds live on.

The Beatles are about to explode on the nation and Elvis is already beginning to seem a bit old hat, but in many ways this view of Hale in about 1960 could date from the mid-thirties, St Peter's Church presiding over a scene of apparently unchanging suburban life. It is pictures like this that make some of us believe that life in the past was somehow more predictable, ordered and secure – but is that really true?

Another classic postcard image, the toddler and nanny in a sun-dappled Bloomsbury Lane, Timperley. What could go wrong in this little world?

—The Altrincham—
Perambulator Carriage Works.

REPAIRS, ADJUSTMENTS AND RENOVATING.

We Specialise in Perambulator Repairs.

Best Workmanship. Lowest Prices.

All Work done on the Premises.

Special Wired on Tyres.

Perambulators of all makes kept in Stock.

Designs made to Order.

Invalid and Spinal Carriages for Sale or Hire.

TELEPHONE 1166.

The Baby Carriage Manufacturing Co.,
30, STAMFORD NEW ROAD, ALTRINCHAM.

Memories of the old 'pram works' in Stamford New Road. It is clear that producing perambulators was a legitimate branch of carriage-making, and that was the way it remained until the 1960s, when the middle classes discovered the convenience of simple carry-cots that could be taken off their wheels and slid into the car. In folk memory at least, the last of the truly impressive prams were often owned by people who might have been expected to have difficulty in affording them.

Barrington Road in about 1920, when little can be heard other than the grasshopper ticking of two bicycle wheels and the clack of a young woman's fashionable shoes.

Section Five
This Sporting Life

Altrincham FC in the 1980/81 season, with the Alliance Premier League trophy which they won in the previous season and retained. Founder members of the APL, they are the only club to date to top the league two seasons running. Back row, left to right: Club coach P. Warburton, B. Whitbread, F. Towers, G. Barrow, J. Connaughton, J. Owens, J. Johnson, Physio J. Evans. Front row: J. Rogers, B. Howard, Captain J. King, Manager A. Sanders, J. Davison, S. Allan, G. Heathcote.

The 1935/36 Altrincham team with the Edward Case trophy, awarded to them for finishing runners-up in the traditionally strong Cheshire League.

Cup fever at Moss Lane: a section of the happy crowd celebrating Altrincham's 6–0 FA Cup win over Scarborough in 1965. The victory gave the club its first Third Round game – against Wolves.

The King – John of that ilk! – receives the FA Trophy at Wembley in May 1978 after Altrincham's 3–1 win over Leatherhead.

Celebrations! The team tours the town after that 1978 Wembley win.

A trip to wonderland: John Hughes puts Altrincham ahead against Everton at Goodison Park in the FA Cup Third Round in January 1975. The Robins drew 1–1 on Merseyside before the First Division club went through 2–0 at Old Trafford. The goalkeeper giving a convincing impression of the proverbial Helpless Custodian is Dai Davies, a quirky Welsh international.

Rugby at Bowdon in the Second World War.

Take that: the expensive attentions of Spurs star Steve Perryman count for nothing as Jeff Johnson equalises for Altrincham at White Hart Lane in the Third Round in January 1979. This was another occasion when a sensational away draw was followed by disappointment in the home replay, for the Robins were no match for Perryman, Ardiles and the rest in a 3–0 beating at Maine Road.

Sporty types from the 2nd Altrincham Boys' Brigade: above, swimmers at Rhyl, 1928; below, a purposeful-looking footballer, Skegness, 1931.

SECTION SIX
CHURCH LIFE

St George's, Altrincham Parish Church, before the rebuilding of 1896–97. The church started life in 1799 as a chapel of ease to Bowdon Parish Church, and was enlarged to cater for Altrincham's growing population in the late 1850s.

St George's Church at the turn of the century.

The Revd E.R. Tarbuck and his wife, pictured in St George's Vicarage grounds in 1903. He was the incumbent from 1902 to 1914.

St Margaret's, Dunham Massey, in the last century. That magnificent spire never came to terms with the bad vibrations of the motor age, and was dismantled as a safety hazard in 1927. Long before then the bells were never rung for fear of bringing the whole structure tumbling down.

The Wesleyan Church in Bank Street, built in 1866 to replace the Chapel Walk building in which John Wesley himself had preached on Easter Monday 1790. Bank Street was the last headquarters of the increasingly amalgamated Methodist congregations in the town before their new church was opened in 1968.

Methodists are admirable people, but as a group they are not associated with soaring flights of fancy. All the more surprising, then, that from 1880 into the second half of the nineteenth century, this should have been their Bowdon base – St Paul's Chapel, inevitably known as the Dome, on Enville Road. It was demolished in the late 1960s, a building impossibly large and expensive to keep up to scratch. No doubt some of the original opponents of the venture were gazing down on the demolition scene from on high and murmuring: 'I told you so'.

Bowdon Parish Church before its major restoration in mid-Victorian times.

Christening party, Bowdon Church, May 1955.

Bowdon Parish Church seen immediately after its massive restoration – a classic example of the Victorians' commitment to church rebuilding. Those who criticise their cavalier attitude to ancient masonry overlook the fact that many of the buildings they 'restored' were in extremely poor repair.

The Church of St John the Evangelist, built for £7,000 in 1865, and seen here in 1900.

St John's from a postcard of the early 1950s, though the picture might have been taken a good many years before that. Even the trees seem little changed from the 1900 view seen opposite.

The Roman Catholic St Vincent de Paul's choir in Railway Street in a May Procession of the 1920s.

Little ones from St Vincent's processing in the 1920s. The picture might be supposed to have been taken at the same time as the one opposite, but in fact it is a year or two later. In the choir picture, the shop in Regent Road next to the Stamford Hotel is Scales' shoe shop, which is holding a closing-down sale. In the photograph above, a clear and newly painted sign proclaims the new owners as Pertinax.

St Vincent's choir assembled for the May Procession of 1933 – a sad day for many, as the well-liked Father Doyle was about to return to Ireland.

St Vincent's May Procession of 1956. In a town that did not observe the Whit walks of Manchester and the Lancashire mill towns, the Catholics' processions were one of the main religious celebrations of the year.

Church parade for the 2nd Altrincham Boys' Brigade, marching past the council offices in Market Street, 1947.

THE PLAY'S THE THING

Sybil Thorndike, accompanied by a daughter who looks as if she wished she were a long way away, opened the Garrick Theatre's three-day Eastern Market in 1930. These charity bazaars were massive fund-raisers in their day – and this one needed to be, for the Garrick were saving hard to build their new Playhouse on Barrington Road. The mayor, A.P. Hill, was a true Garrick stalwart and had in fact donated the land for the new theatre.

The Playhouse shortly after its opening in 1932.

A.P. Hill as Jones in *The Silver Box*, the Garrick's first production, at the Public Hall in March 1914.

In Dame Wendy Hiller, Altrincham's Club Theatre, founded in 1896 and currently planning some exciting centenary celebrations, has had an enthusiastic and supportive president over the years. She is seen here in the 1938 film version of Shaw's *Pygmalion*, playing Eliza to the Professor Higgins of Rex Harrison. He of course revived the role for the 1960s stage and film productions of *My Fair Lady*.

Garrick staff preparing for the 1923 production of the play *If* – a wonderfully stagey picture, and a little work of art in itself.

The Garrick's production of *When the Crash Comes*, October 1934, with a cast that included two giants of the society's history, A.P. Hill and Lloyd Birch.

The BBC now describe *The Grove Family* as a mid-1950s TV soap opera, though at the time it was surely seen more as an entertaining comedy. Altrincham had a special interest in it since Ruth Dunning, who played Mrs Grove, cut her theatrical teeth at the Garrick. She is seen second from the left on the front row – next to Nancy Roberts, who played the dreadful Gran.

The Garrick's production for the coronation of 1953 was Noël Coward's *Cavalcade*, a massive undertaking which also marked the society's 40th anniversary. Seen here are two scenes from an endless list of tableaux, the soldiers below stirring memories of the film choreographer Busby Berkeley's 'My Forgotten Man' routine.

The dress rehearsal of the Garrick's *Dick Whittington*, Christmas 1965, with the principal girl still in her Swinging Sixties street clothes and the principal boy laying more stress on rehearsal than dress. From left to right are Charles Foster as Alderman Fitzwarren; Anne McKenna as Alice; Michael Oliver as Dame Cicely Suett; Peter Dudley as the Cat; Neville Roby as Marmaduke Bung; and Pat Thompson as Dick. The eagle-eyed will immediately recognise the Cat as the actor who went on to play Ivy's first husband in *Coronation Street*.

Tom Jones was the Garrick's choice to mark the Queen's silver jubilee in 1977. Seen here are Belinda Mencel as Sophia and Peter Jackson as Lord Fellamar.

The Regal on Manchester Road could seat 2,000 and was regarded as one of the Manchester area's finest cinemas, Compton organ and all. It was opened by Lord Stamford in 1931, and was destroyed by fire early in 1956. Perhaps there is a grain of comfort in this, since it would be sad to see such a place in use as a discount warehouse or snooker club.

The Hippodrome in Stamford Street was a latecomer to the music hall and variety circuit. It opened just before the First World War, and though good turns and bad trooped through its stage door for four decades or so, by the mid-fifties variety was proving no match for TV. It became a very comfortable cinema, latterly in the Cannon chain, before bowing out in 1986. The revival of interest in going to the pictures in the ten years since then prompts the thought that timing was never the Hippodrome's strong point.

They made their own fun at the Old Packet House, Broadheath, in the early years of the nineteenth century, though Wilson's Newton Heath Ales doubtless helped the cause. F. Neil was the photographer who discovered that whatever the picture, a gang of little boys would intrude into it somehow.

MEET THE FOLKS

The Altrincham area ARP ambulance in June 1943, with Mrs Isabel Fairley, centre, and colleagues. They are beside the Picture Theatre, where the Station House office block now stands – a cinema for which Hitler held no fears, but which succumbed to commercial pressures in 1966.

Old people's treat at the Literary Institute to mark George V's coronation, June 1911. The streamers look a great deal more cheerful than most of the faces beneath them.

Altrincham lads on their motorbike in Rhyl, 1928.

Eustace George Parker JP – a jeweller
on the corner of Stamford New Road
and Grafton Street who made the
mayoral chain, and had the honour of
wearing it in 1889–90.

David Morrison, auctioneer, accountant and
estate agent, who was mayor in the mid-
1890s. His son Stanley was similarly honoured
in 1926–27.

Altrincham flappers at Withernsea, 1930.

2nd Altrincham Boys' Brigade ready for soccer, Skegness, 1931.

Salvation Army sewing circle, George Street, Second World War. The three girls in the centre are Connie Roberts, Lilian Williams and Olive Clark. 'You didn't have to be in the Salvation Army,' says Lilian Williams, now Mrs Nash. 'But Miss Cutts, who took the sewing circle, was always mithering me to join.'

Culcheth Hall school party to France, Ypres, April 1936.

Broadheath factory workers, possibly radium or blacking works, early 1930s.

George Street Salvation Army Indian club swingers and skippers, *c.* 1940. Miss Cutts, seated in the centre, led the older girls in their Indian club routines and the little ones in skipping.

Factory girls Joyce Langford and Lilian Williams taking a break from work at Cook and Co.'s, off Moss Lane, towards the end of the Second World War. Cook's wartime production was largely devoted to quick-release pins for parachutes, and percussion and primer caps for guns.

Sunday best: Broadheath factory workers on a trip to Ilkley, Yorkshire, early 1930s.

ACKNOWLEDGEMENTS

Thanks for the loan of photographs and other much appreciated help when this book was first published in 1995 are due to:

The staff of Altrincham Library • Altrincham FC
Altrincham Garrick Society • 2nd Altrincham Boys' Brigade • Janet Bradshaw
Betsy Cheeseman • Culcheth Old Girls' Union • George Fairley • Jean Hamer
Anne Hurst • Chris Jenner • Pamela Knox • Loreto Convent Grammar School Mrs
Montague, St Vincent's Church • Basil Morrison • Brian and Lilian Nash
Ian Roberts • John Starkey • Terry Surridge • Miriam Tyler

Paper Hanging Establishment,

RAILWAY STREET.
(OPPOSITE THE BOWDON RAILWAY STATION,)
ALTRINCHAM.

WILLIAM JEPSON,

Begs leave to thank the Public of Altrincham, Bowdon, and the neighbourhood. for the very liberal support he has received since the opening of his Establishment, and hopes by strict attention to business to merit a share of their patronage.

N. B.—*Agent for HEYWOOD & Co's celebrated Paper Hangings the* **Cheapest House in the Kingdom.** *Patterns and Paper Hangers sent to all parts of the Country.*

SCHOOLS SUPPLIED WITH STATIONERY AT WHOLESALE PRICES.

LETTER-PRESS PRINTING & BOOK-BINDING

Executed on the Premises in a first-rate style. W. P. having recently added to his Office a new Printing Press capable of producing impressions for Posting Bills, Hand Bills, Circulars Catalogues, Invoices, Check Books, &c. &c.

AGENT for all the London and Manchester Newspapers, which are delivered in Altrincham and Bowdon every morning (Sundays excepted) at 7 30.

CIRCULATING LIBRARY.

WIGAN & LEIGH BEST HOUSE COALS,
ALTRINCHAM WHARF.

HENRY SERVICE, AGENT,
BOWDON.

HENRY KINSEY,
BUTCHER,
MARKET PLACE, ALTRINCHAM,

A final reminder of another world nearly a century and a half ago – the Altrincham of 1855, a heady cocktail of the familiar and the very, very strange.